Beginner's Guide to
Crocodile Stitch

LEISURE ARTS, INC. • Maumelle, Arkansas

EDITORIAL STAFF

Vice President of Editorial: Susan White Sullivan
Creative Art Director: Katherine Laughlin
Publications Director: Leah Lampirez
Technical Writer/Editor: Cathy Hardy
Associate Technical Editors: Linda A. Daley,
 Sarah J. Green, and Lois J. Long
Editorial Writer: Susan Frantz Wiles
Art Category Manager: Lora Puls
Graphic Artist: Jacqueline Breazeal
Prepress Technician: Stephanie Johnson
Contributing Photographers: Jason Masters and
 Ken West
Contributing Photo Stylist: Lori Wenger

BUSINESS STAFF

President and Chief Executive Officer: Fred F. Pruss
Senior Vice President of Operations: Jim Dittrich
Vice President of Retail Sales: Martha Adams
Chief Financial Officer: Tiffany P. Childers
Controller: Teresa Eby
Information Technology Director: Brian Roden
Director of E-Commerce: Mark Hawkins
Manager of E-Commerce: Robert Young

We have made every effort to ensure that these
instructions are accurate and complete. We
cannot, however, be responsible for human
error, typographical mistakes, or variations in
individual work.

Our thanks go to Cobblestone & Vine in The Heights
in Little Rock, Arkansas, for allowing us to photograph
our designs in their beautiful home furnishings store.

ISBN-13: 978-1-4647-1651-5

Have you been eager to crochet some of the
gorgeous Crocodile Stitch designs you've been
seeing, but you felt intimidated by those dense, dimensional
layers? Fear no more, because this book breaks it all down
to super-easy steps that anyone can learn! Clear photos and
instructions are given throughout, and free online videos offer
extra help with the techniques. Turn to page 4 to get started.

Meet the Designer

Crocodile Stitch is easy to learn and
fun to crochet, says Lisa Gentry. But
there is also a third reason she chose it
as a design topic – over the years, she
has seen a few alligators in the lake
near her home in Louisiana!

A native of Germany and a crocheter
since first grade, Lisa came to the
attention of the yarn industry after being awarded the title of Fastest
Crocheter by the Guinness World Records in 2005. She was also later
named America's fastest knitter by the Craft Yarn Council.

Since then, her knit and crochet designs have been prominently
featured in top magazines and published in nearly 20 Leisure Arts
books. Topics include chain knitting (a technique Lisa invented),
ribbon crochet, women's sweaters, celebrity baby fashions, celebrity
slouchy beanies for the family, urban hats made with The Knook®,
cowls, neckwear, and more.

Look for Lisa's books on LeisureArts.com. For more about
her designs, visit Ravelry.com and her company website,
HookAndNeedleDesigns.com.

Beginner's Guide to CROCODILE STITCH

Are you interested in learning a unique stitch that's very versatile? With its eye-catching layers of "scales," Crocodile Stitch is a fun choice that will add interest to lots of different projects, from fashions to home décor.

You'll be surprised how easy it is to learn Crocodile Stitch, using our detailed photographs and step-by-step instructions, plus online technique videos. Best of all, as you practice this new stitch, you'll create beautiful projects for you, your friends, and your home.

Let's get started!

Getting Started

The best way to learn Crocodile Stitch is to **build your skills a little at a time**. In this book, we **start with an easy bracelet** on page 6 to teach you how to make the individual Scales of Crocodile Stitch. **Up-close photos** show you every step, and **clear instructions** walk you through the whole process. We've even created **free online videos** to help you; orange camera icons 🎥 throughout the book let you know when there are videos to watch at www.LeisureArts.com/6377.

After practicing the Scales and making the bracelet, you'll learn how to work in **rounds** to make Scales for an amazing pair of mitts (page 10) and then how to work **rows** of Scales to embellish both ends of a fun scarf (page 16). More projects let you practice all these techniques and pick up additional knowledge. You're going to love the versatility of Crocodile Stitch!

Supplies

You only need basic supplies such as **yarn** and a **crochet hook**. A shopping list is provided with each project. Since gauge is important in some of the projects to ensure that it is the desired size, you'll want a **tape measure** as well. A **yarn needle** is used to weave in yarn ends and for sewing.

Scale Bracelet

When you break it down, Crocodile Stitch is simply a series of individual Scales. Each Scale is formed by making a ring and then working two groups of double crochets into it. This bracelet is a great beginner project because you learn how to make Scales in a continuous strip. Make the strip as long as you need, and stack several bracelets for a fun look.

◖■■□⊃ EASY

Finished Size: 1½" (3.75 cm) wide
8 Scales - 7½" (19 cm) long
9 Scales - 8¼" (21 cm) long

SHOPPING LIST

Yarn (Medium Weight)

☐ 8 or 9 Scales - 16 yards (14.5 meters) **each**

Crochet Hook

☐ Size H (5 mm) **or** size needed for gauge

Additional Supplies

☐ Button to fit button loop

☐ Matching thread

☐ Sewing needle

GAUGE INFORMATION

In Crocodile Stitch,
   One Scale = 1½" (3.75 cm) wide

INSTRUCTIONS

 **FIRST SCALE**

Ch 4, dc in fourth ch from hook to form a ring.

To work into the ring, begin by working around the post of the dc just made. You can work over the beginning end at the same time *(Fig. 1a)*, then continue working around the beginning ch.

Fig. 1a

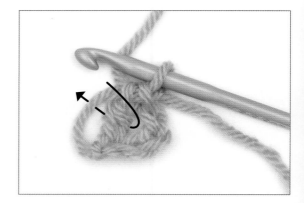

Ch 1, work (5 dc, ch 1, 5 dc, slip st) in the ring to form the first Scale *(Fig. 1b)*: 10 dc.

Fig. 1b

▶ NEXT SCALE

Ch 3, dc in center of Scale just made to form the foundation for the next Scale *(Fig. 2a)*.

Fig. 2a

Ch 1, work 5 dc down post of last dc made *(Fig. 2b)*.

Fig. 2b

Ch 1, rotate piece holding the yarn and hook **behind** previous Scale *(Fig. 2c)*.

Fig. 2c

Work 5 dc up the beginning ch-3 to form a Scale, slip st in same sp *(Fig. 2d)*.

Fig. 2d

The Bracelet is made with the **wrong** side facing. The Scales will overlap each other on the **right** side *(Fig. 2e)*.

Fig. 2e   **Right Side**

Continue making Scales, following the instructions for the Next Scale, for a total of 8 or 9 Scales, **or** to your desired length.

Button Loop: Ch 6, slip st in center of Scale just made; finish off.

Sew a button to the right side of First Scale.

VERY GOOD!

The bracelet has introduced you to
the basics of Crocodile Stitch. Now let's learn
how to make Scales working in the round
as you make the Fanciful Mitts, page 10.

Fanciful Mitts

Now that you know the basics of making Scales, let's learn to work them in layers on Foundation Rounds. You'll love how easily this technique creates a lush fabric. These mitts have cozy layers of Scales all around the hand and deep cuffs with a pretty stitch pattern.

 EASY

SHOPPING LIST

Yarn (Medium Weight)

[3.5 ounces, 280 yards (100 grams, 256 meters) per skein]:

☐ Variegated - 1 skein

[5 ounces, 256 yards (141 grams, 234 meters) per skein]:

☐ Purple - 1 skein

Crochet Hooks

☐ Size H (5 mm) **and**

☐ Size I (5.5 mm)

or sizes needed for gauge

SIZE INFORMATION

Finished Size:

Hand Circumference - 7{8}"/18{20.5} cm

Length - 13" (33 cm)

Size Note: We have printed the instructions for the sizes in different colors to make it easier for you to find:

· Size Small in Blue

· Size Medium in Pink

Instructions in Black apply to both sizes.

GAUGE INFORMATION

In Crocodile Stitch,

with larger size hook and Variegated,

3 Scales = $3^{1}/_{2}$" (9 cm),

10 rnds = $3^{1}/_{4}$" (8.25 cm)

In Arm pattern,

with smaller size hook and Purple,

2 repeats = 2" (5 cm),

4 rows/rnds = $2^{1}/_{4}$" (5.75 cm)

Gauge Swatch: $2^{1}/_{4}$" (5.75 cm) square

With smaller size hook and Purple, ch 11.

Row 1: (Dc, ch 1, dc) in fifth ch from hook **(first 3 skipped chs count as first dc)**, skip next ch, dc in next ch, skip next ch, (dc, ch 1, dc) in next ch, skip next ch, dc in last ch: 7 dc and 2 chs.

Rows 2-4: Ch 3 **(counts as first dc)**, turn; ★ skip next dc, (dc, ch 1, dc) in next ch-1 sp, skip next dc, dc in next dc; repeat from ★ once **more**. Finish off.

INSTRUCTIONS
HAND

With larger size hook and Variegated, ch 30{35}; being careful **not** to twist ch, join with slip st to form a ring.

RND 1 - Foundation Rnd:

Ch 3 (**counts as first dc, now and throughout**), dc in same st, ch 1, skip next 2 chs, dc in next ch, ch 1, skip next ch, ★ 2 dc in next ch, ch 1, skip next 2 chs, dc in next ch, ch 1, skip next ch; repeat from ★ around; join with slip st to first dc: 6{7} 2-dc groups, 6{7} dc, and 12{14} chs.

Each Scale is worked around both posts of a 2-dc group on the Foundation Rnd, working down the first post and up the second post, rotating the piece as instructed.

📹 RND 2 - Scale Rnd:

Ch 3, work 4 dc down post of first dc, then rotate piece (*Figs. 3a & b*).

Fig. 3a

Fig. 3b

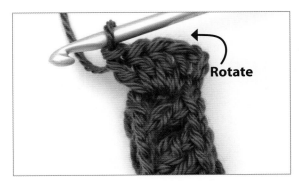

Rotate

Ch 2, work 5 dc up post of next dc in 2-dc group to form a Scale (*Figs. 3c & d*).

Fig. 3c

Fig. 3d

Skip next ch, slip st in next dc (*Fig. 3e*). The Scale will lie flat against the Foundation Rnd.

Fig. 3e

★ Skip next ch, work 5 dc down post of next dc (first dc of next 2-dc group), ch 2, rotate piece and work 5 dc up post of next dc (second dc of 2-dc group), skip next ch, slip st in next dc; repeat from ★ around to last ch; do **not** join: 6{7} Scales.

All of the Scales are on the **right** side and the single dc of the Foundation Rnd is **behind** the Scales.

🎥 RND 3 - Foundation Rnd:

Ch 3, dc in same dc as last slip st made, ch 1, dc in center of next Scale *(Fig. 4a)*.

Fig. 4a

Ch 1, ★ 2 dc in next slip st (between Scales) *(Fig. 4b)*, ch 1, dc in center of next Scale, ch 1; repeat from ★ around; join with slip st to first dc: 6{7} 2-dc groups, 6{7} dc, and 12{14} chs.

Fig. 4b

RND 4 - Scale Rnd:

Ch 3, work 4 dc down post of first dc, ch 2, rotate piece and work 5 dc up post of next dc, skip next ch, slip st in next dc, ★ skip next ch, work 5 dc down post of next dc, ch 2, rotate piece and work 5 dc up post of next dc, skip next ch, slip st in next dc; repeat from ★ around to last ch; do **not** join: 6{7} Scales.

Each Scale overlaps the Scale on the previous Scale Round, and is centered between two Scales.

Rnds 5-10: Repeat Rnds 3 and 4, 3 times.

Finish off.

GREAT JOB!

Now you know how to make the Crocodile Stitch worked in rounds!

THUMB OPENING

Row 1: With **right** side facing and using smaller size hook, join Purple with slip st in center of any Scale on last rnd; ch 1, 2 sc in same sp, 2{1} sc in next slip st, (3 sc in center of next Scale, 2 sc in next slip st) around; do **not** join: 29{33} sc.

Row 2: Ch 1, turn; sc in each sc around; do **not** finish off.

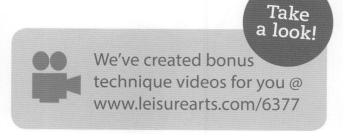

Take a look!

We've created bonus technique videos for you @ www.leisurearts.com/6377

ARM

Rnd 1: Ch 3, turn; ★ skip next sc, (dc, ch 1, dc) in next sc, skip next sc, dc in next sc; repeat from ★ around, ch 3; join with slip st to first dc: 22{25} dc, 7{8} ch-1 sps, and one ch-3 sp.

Rnd 2: Ch 3, do **not** turn; ★ skip next dc, (dc, ch 1, dc) in next ch-1 sp, skip next dc, dc in next dc; repeat from ★ around, (dc, ch 1, dc) in last ch-3 sp; join with slip st to first dc: 24{27} dc and 8{9} ch-1 sps.

Rnd 3: Ch 3, skip next dc, (dc, ch 1, dc) in next ch-1 sp, skip next dc, ★ dc in next dc, skip next dc, (dc, ch 1, dc) in next ch-1 sp, skip next dc; repeat from ★ around; join with slip st to first dc.

Repeat Rnd 3 for pattern until piece measures approximately 12½" (32 cm) from beginning.

Last Rnd: Ch 1, (sc, 3 dc, sc) in each ch-1 sp around; join with slip st to first sc, finish off.

Make one more mitt so you'll have a pair, then go on to learn how to work the Crocodile Stitch while working in rows. The Bordered Scarf, page 16, is just the project for that.

Bordered Scarf

When you want a flat fabric of Crocodile Stitch, you'll need to know how to work in rows. Learn how with this Bordered Scarf. It is crocheted in two identical pieces and joined together in the middle.

EASY

Finished Size:
6" wide x 70½" long (15 cm x 179 cm)

SHOPPING LIST

Yarn (Medium Weight)

[5 ounces, 251 yards (142 grams, 230 meters) per skein]:
- ☐ 2 skeins

Crochet Hooks
- ☐ Size I (5.5 mm) **and**
- ☐ Size J (6 mm)

  or sizes needed for gauge

Additional Supplies
- ☐ Yarn needle

GAUGE

In Crocodile Stitch Border pattern,
with smaller size hook,

   5 Scales = 6" (15.25 cm),

   6 rows = 2¹/₂" (6.25 cm)

In Body pattern, with larger size hook,

   8 sts = 2" (5 cm),

   8 rows = 4¹/₂" (11.5 cm)

Gauge Swatch: 3¹/₄" wide x 2³/₄" high

   (8.25 cm x 7 cm)

With larger size hook, ch 15.

Row 1: Dc in fourth ch from hook **(3 skipped chs count as first dc)** and in each ch across: 13 dc.

Rows 2-5: Work same as Body Rows 3-6, page 23.

Finish off.

——— STITCH GUIDE ———

PUFF ST (uses one st)

★ YO, insert hook in st indicated, YO and pull up a loop even with loop on hook; repeat from ★ once **more**, YO and draw through all 5 loops on hook.

INSTRUCTIONS

FIRST HALF

CROCODILE STITCH BORDER

With smaller size hook, ch 28.

ROW 1 - Foundation Row (Wrong side)**:**

Dc in fourth ch from hook (**3 skipped chs count as first dc**), ★ ch 1, skip next 2 chs, dc in next ch, ch 1, skip next 2 chs, 2 dc in next ch; repeat from ★ across *(Fig. 5)*: 5 2-dc groups, 4 dc, and 8 chs.

Fig. 5

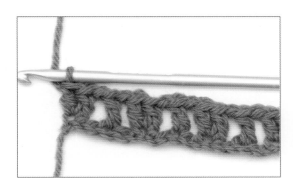

Each Scale is worked around both posts of a 2-dc group on the Foundation Row, working down the first post and up the second post, rotating the piece as instructed.

■ ROW 2 - Scale Row:

Ch 1, work 5 dc down post of last dc made working over the beginning end at the same time, then rotate Foundation Row *(Fig. 6a)*.

Fig. 6a

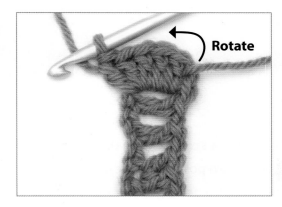

Ch 1, work 5 dc up post of next dc to form a Scale *(Figs. 6b & c)*.

Fig. 6b

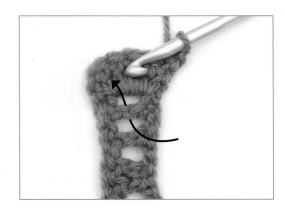

Fig. 6c

★ Skip next ch, slip st in next dc *(Fig. 6d)*. The Scale will lie flat against the Foundation Row.

Fig. 6d

To work a Scale around the next 2-dc group, work 5 dc down post of next dc *(Fig. 7a)*, ch 1, rotate piece and work 5 dc up post of next dc *(Fig. 7b)*.

Fig. 7a

Fig. 7b

All of the Scales are on the **right** side of the Scarf *(Fig. 8a)* and the single dc on the Foundation Row is **behind** the Scales *(Fig. 8b)*.

Fig. 8a

Right Side

Fig. 8b

Wrong Side

Repeat from ★ across, slip st around post of same dc: 5 Scales.

◼️ ROW 3 - Foundation Row:

Ch 4 **(counts as first dc plus ch 1, now and throughout)**, 2 dc in next slip st (between Scales) *(Fig. 9a)*, ch 1, dc in center of next Scale *(Fig. 9b)*, ★ ch 1, 2 dc in next slip st, ch 1, dc in center of next Scale; repeat from ★ across: 4 2-dc groups, 5 dc, and 8 chs.

Fig. 9a

Fig. 9b

ROW 4 - Scale Row:

Turn; slip st in first dc, ★ skip next ch, work 5 dc down post of next dc *(Fig. 10a)*, ch 1, rotate piece and work 5 dc up post of next dc *(Fig. 10b)*, skip next ch, slip st in next dc *(Fig. 10c)*; repeat from ★ across: 4 Scales.

Fig. 10a

Fig. 10b

Fig. 10c

Each Scale overlaps the Scale on the previous Scale Row and is centered between two Scales.

ROW 5 - Foundation Row:

Ch 3 **(counts as first dc, now and throughout)**, turn; dc in first slip st, ★ ch 1, dc in center of next Scale, ch 1, 2 dc in next slip st; repeat from ★ across: 5 2-dc groups, 4 dc, and 8 chs.

ROW 6 - Scale Row:

Ch 1, work 5 dc down post of last dc made, ch 1, rotate piece and work 5 dc up post of next dc, ★ skip next ch, slip st in next dc, skip next ch, work 5 dc down post of next dc, ch 1, rotate piece and work 5 dc up post of next dc; repeat from ★ across, slip st around post of same dc: 5 Scales.

Rows 7-14: Repeat Rows 3-6 twice.

Do **not** finish off.

Well Done!

Now you know how to make many projects using the Crocodile Stitch! The Body is made by working a pattern stitch to give your scarf added texture.

BODY

Change to larger size hook.

Row 1: Ch 1, turn; 4 sc in center of first Scale, 2 sc in next slip st, ★ 2 sc in center of next Scale, 2 sc in next slip st; repeat from ★ across to last Scale, 3 sc in center of last Scale: 21 sc.

Row 2: Ch 3, turn; dc in next sc and in each sc across.

Row 3: Ch 3, turn; dc in next dc, ch 1, ★ skip next dc, work Puff St in next dc, ch 1; repeat from ★ across to last 3 dc, skip next dc, dc in last 2 dc: 8 Puff Sts, 9 ch-1 sps, and 4 dc.

Row 4: Ch 3, turn; dc in next dc and in each ch-1 sp and each Puff St across to last 2 dc, dc in last 2 dc: 21 dc.

Row 5: Ch 3, turn; dc in next dc, ch 1, ★ skip next dc, dc in next dc, ch 1; repeat from ★ across to last 3 dc, skip next dc, dc in last 2 dc: 12 dc and 9 ch-1 sps.

Row 6: Ch 3, turn; dc in next dc and in each ch-1 sp and each dc across: 21 dc.

Repeat Rows 3-6 for pattern until Body measures approximately 34¹/₂" (87.5 cm) from beginning, ending by working Row 3.

Last Row: Ch 1, turn; sc in first dc and in each ch-1 sp and each st across; finish off: 21 sc.

SECOND HALF

Work same as First Half until Body measures approximately 35¹/₂" (90 cm) from beginning, ending by working Row 5 of Body.

Last Row: Ch 1, turn; sc in first dc and in each ch-1 sp and each dc across; finish off leaving a long end for sewing: 21 sc.

Whipstitch last row of both pieces together *(Fig. 16a, page 47)*.

Congratulations!

All of the remaining projects in this book use the same techniques that you learned while making the mitts and the scarf. Enjoy your newfound skill!

Plush Pillow

Only the front of this pretty pillow is worked in Crocodile Stitch; the back is all quick and easy double crochet stitches. To plump it up, insert a ready-made pillow or pillow form, or sew your own pillow form and stuff it with fiberfill.

 **EASY**

Finished Size:
18¹/₂" wide x 16" high (47 cm x 40.5 cm)

SHOPPING LIST

Yarn (Medium Weight)
[4 ounces, 212 yards (113 grams, 194 meters) per skein]:
- ☐ 4 skeins

Crochet Hook
- ☐ Size I (5.5 mm) **or** size needed for gauge

Additional Supplies
- ☐ 18¹/₂" x 16" (47 cm x 40.5 cm) Pillow form **or** 20" x 33" (51" cm x 84 cm) fabric **and** polyester fiberfill
- ☐ Yarn needle

GAUGE INFORMATION

In Crocodile Stitch,

   3 Scales and 10 rows = 4" (10 cm)

In Back pattern,

   11 dc and 7 rows = 3¹/₂" (9 cm)

Gauge Swatch: 3¹/₂" (9 cm) square

Ch 13.

Row 1: Dc in fourth ch from hook (**3 skipped chs count as first dc**) and in each ch across: 11 dc.

Rows 2-7: Ch 3 (**counts as first dc**), turn; dc in next dc and in each dc across.

Finish off.

INSTRUCTIONS
CROCODILE STITCH FRONT

Ch 82.

Row 1 (Foundation row - Wrong side)**:** Dc in fourth ch from hook (**3 skipped chs count as first dc**), ★ ch 1, skip next 2 chs, dc in next ch, ch 1, skip next 2 chs, 2 dc in next ch; repeat from ★ across *(Fig. 5, page 19)*: 14 2-dc groups, 13 dc, and 26 chs.

Row 2 (Scale row)**:** Ch 1, work 5 dc down post of last dc made working over the beginning end at the same time, ch 1, rotate Foundation Row and work 5 dc up post of next dc to form a Scale *(Figs. 6a-c, page 19)*, ★ skip next ch, slip st in next dc, skip next ch, work 5 dc down post of next dc, ch 1, rotate piece and work 5 dc up post of next dc *(Fig. 6d and Figs. 7a & b, page 20)*; repeat from ★ across, slip st around post of same dc: 14 Scales.

Row 3 (Foundation row)**:** Ch 4 **(counts as first dc plus ch 1, now and throughout)**, 2 dc in next slip st (between Scales), ch 1, dc in center of next Scale *(Figs. 9a & b, page 21)*, ★ ch 1, 2 dc in next slip st, ch 1, dc in center of next Scale; repeat from ★ across: 13 2-dc groups, 14 dc, and 26 chs.

Row 4 (Scale row)**:** Turn; slip st in first dc, ★ skip next ch, work 5 dc down post of next dc, ch 1, rotate piece and work 5 dc up post of next dc, skip next ch, slip st in next dc *(Figs. 10a-c, page 22)*; repeat from ★ across: 13 Scales.

Row 5 (Foundation row)**:** Ch 3 **(counts as first dc, now and throughout)**, turn; dc in first slip st, ★ ch 1, dc in center of next Scale, ch 1, 2 dc in next slip st; repeat from ★ across: 14 2-dc groups, 13 dc, and 26 chs.

Row 6 (Scale row)**:** Ch 1, work 5 dc down post of last dc made, ch 1, rotate piece and work 5 dc up post of next dc, ★ skip next ch, slip st in next dc, skip next ch, work 5 dc down post of next dc, ch 1, rotate piece and work 5 dc up post of next dc; repeat from ★ across, slip st around post of same dc: 14 Scales.

Repeat Rows 3-6 for pattern until Front measures approximately 16" (40.5 cm) from beginning, ending by working Row 6; do **not** finish off.

BACK

Row 1: Ch 1, turn; 3 sc in center of first Scale, 3 sc in next slip st, 2 sc in center of next Scale, (2 sc in next slip st, 2 sc in center of next Scale) across to last slip st, 3 sc in last slip st, 3 sc in center of last Scale: 58 sc.

Row 2: Ch 3, turn; dc in next st and in each st across.

Repeat Row 2 until Back measures same as Front; finish off.

If desired, using Pillow cover as a guide, make a pillow form or cover a purchased pillow form.

With **wrong** sides together, whipstitch across 2 sides *(Figs. 16a & b, page 47)*; insert pillow form and whipstitch across remaining side.

Take a look!

We've created bonus videos for you @ www.leisurearts.com/6377

Luxurious Cowl

Because this cowl is worked in the round, there's no
finishing needed after you complete the Crocodile Stitches.
A soft multicolor yarn provides the beautiful color variations.

 EASY

Finished Size:
7¹/₂" high x 28³/₄" circumference
(19 cm x 73 cm)

SHOPPING LIST

Yarn (Medium Weight)

[3.5 ounces, 280 yards (100 grams, 256 meters) per skein]:

☐ 2 skeins

Crochet Hook

☐ Size I (5.5 mm) **or** size needed for gauge

GAUGE INFORMATION

In Crocodile Stitch,

   2 Scales = 2¹/₂" (6.25 cm),

   6 rows/rnds = 1³/₄" (4.5 cm)

Gauge Swatch: 2¹/₂" wide x 1³/₄" high

   (6.25 cm x 4.5 cm)

Ch 13.

Row 1: Dc in fourth ch from hook **(3 skipped chs count as first dc)**, ch 1, skip next 2 chs, dc in next ch, ch 1, skip next 2 chs, 2 dc in next ch, ch 1, skip next 2 chs, dc in last ch: 2 2-dc groups, 2 dc, and 3 chs.

Rows 2 and 3: Ch 3 **(counts as first dc)**, turn; dc in first dc, ch 1, dc in center of next 2-dc group (sp between dc), ch 1, skip next ch, 2 dc in next dc, ch 1, dc in center of last 2-dc group.

Finish off.

INSTRUCTIONS

Ch 138; being careful **not** to twist ch, join with slip st to form a ring.

Rnd 1 (Foundation rnd)**:** Ch 3 **(counts as first dc, now and throughout)**, dc in same st, ch 1, skip next 2 chs, dc in next ch, ch 1, skip next 2 chs, ★ 2 dc in next ch, ch 1, skip next 2 chs, dc in next ch, ch 1, skip next 2 chs; repeat from ★ around; join with slip st to first dc: 23 2-dc groups, 23 dc, and 46 chs.

Rnd 2 (Scale rnd)**:** Ch 3, work 4 dc down post of first dc, ch 1, rotate piece and work 5 dc up post of next dc to form a Scale, skip next ch, slip st in next dc *(Figs. 3a-e, page 13)*, ★ skip next ch, work 5 dc down post of next dc, ch 1, rotate piece and work 5 dc up post of next dc, skip next ch, slip st in next dc; repeat from ★ around to last ch; do **not** join: 23 Scales.

Rnd 3 (Foundation rnd)**:** Ch 3, dc in same dc as last slip st made, ch 1, dc in center of next Scale, ch 1, ★ 2 dc in next slip st (between Scales), ch 1, dc in center of next Scale, ch 1; repeat from ★ around *(Figs. 4a & b, page 14)*; join with slip st to first dc: 23 2-dc groups, 23 dc, and 46 chs.

Rnds 4-26: Repeat Rnds 2 and 3, 11 times; then repeat Rnd 2 once **more**: 23 Scales.

Finish off.

Embellished Bag

This shoulder bag is worked in the round, so all you have to do is join the bottom edges and add the strap. We also lined our bag and fortified the strap with grosgrain ribbon. A pretty flower adds the finishing touch.

 **EASY**

Finished Size:
10½" wide x 9½" high
(26.5 cm x 24 cm)

SHOPPING LIST

Yarn (Medium Weight) 🧶 4 MEDIUM

[3 ounces, 145 yards (85 grams, 133 meters) per skein]:

☐ Main Color - 3 skeins

☐ Contrasting Color - 20 yards (18.5 meters)

Crochet Hooks

☐ Size H (5 mm) **and**

☐ Size I (5.5 mm)

or size needed for gauge

Additional Supplies

☐ Yarn needle

Optional:

☐ Fabric for lining - 11½" x 20" (29 cm x 51 cm)

☐ Grosgrain ribbon for strap - 1½ yards (1.37 meters)

☐ Sewing needle

☐ Matching thread

GAUGE INFORMATION

In Crocodile Stitch,

   with larger size hook,

   4 Scales = 6" (15 cm),

   6 rows/rnds = $2\frac{1}{4}$" (5.75 cm)

Gauge Swatch: $2\frac{1}{4}$" (5.75 cm) square

With larger size hook, ch 13.

Row 1: Dc in fourth ch from hook (**3 skipped chs count as first dc**), ch 1, skip next 2 chs, dc in next ch, ch 1, skip next 2 chs, 2 dc in next ch, ch 1, skip next 2 chs, dc in last ch: 2 2-dc groups, 2 dc, and 3 chs.

Rows 2-4: Ch 3 (**counts as first dc**), turn; dc in first dc, ch 1, dc in center of next 2-dc group (sp between dc), ch 1, skip next ch, 2 dc in next dc, ch 1, dc in center of last 2-dc group.

Finish off.

INSTRUCTIONS
BODY

With larger size hook, using Main Color, and leaving a long end for sewing, ch 84; being careful **not** to twist ch, join with slip st to form a ring.

Rnd 1: Ch 1, sc in each ch around; join with slip st to first sc: 84 sc.

Rnd 2 (Foundation rnd)**:** Ch 3 (**counts as first dc, now and throughout**), dc in same st, ch 1, skip next 2 sc, dc in next sc, ch 1, skip next 2 sc, ★ 2 dc in next sc, ch 1, skip next 2 sc, dc in next sc, ch 1, skip next 2 sc; repeat from ★ around; join with slip st to first dc: 14 2-dc groups, 14 dc, and 28 chs.

Rnd 3 (Scale rnd)**:** Ch 3, work 4 dc down post of first dc, ch 1, rotate piece and work 5 dc up post of next dc to form Scale, skip next ch, slip st in next dc (*Figs. 3a-e, page 13*), ★ skip next ch, work 5 dc down post of next dc, ch 1, rotate piece and work 5 dc up post of next dc, skip next ch, slip st in next dc; repeat from ★ around to last ch; do **not** join: 14 Scales.

Rnd 4 (Foundation rnd)**:** Ch 3, dc in same dc as last slip st made, ch 1, dc in center of next Scale, ch 1, ★ 2 dc in next slip st (between Scales), ch 1, dc in center of next Scale, ch 1; repeat from ★ around (*Figs. 4a & b, page 14*); join with slip st to first dc: 14 2-dc groups, 14 dc, and 28 chs.

Rnds 5-25: Repeat Rnds 3 and 4, 10 times; then repeat Rnd 3 once **more**: 14 Scales.

Rnd 26: Ch 1, 2 sc in each slip st and in center of each Scale around; join with slip st to first sc: 56 sc.

Rnd 27: Ch 1, sc in each sc around; join with slip st to first sc, finish off.

Flatten Body and 🎥 whipstitch bottom edge closed using long end (*Fig. 16a, page 47*).

STRAP

With smaller size hook, using Main Color, and leaving a long end for sewing, ch 6.

Row 1: Sc in second ch from hook and in each ch across: 5 sc.

Row 2: Ch 1, turn; sc in each sc across.

Repeat Row 2 until Strap measures approximately 42" (106.5 cm) from beginning ch; finish off leaving a long end for sewing.

Sew each end of Strap to inside top edge of Body at opposite sides.

If desired, sew grosgrain ribbon to **inner** side of Strap to prevent it from stretching.

FLOWER

With smaller size hook, using Contrasting Color, and leaving a long end for sewing, ch 4; join with slip st to form a ring.

Rnd 1 (Right side)**:** Ch 1, (sc in ring, ch 2) 6 times; join with slip st to first sc: 6 ch-2 sps.

Rnd 2: Ch 1, (sc, hdc, dc, hdc, sc) in each ch-2 sp around; join with slip st to first sc: 6 petals.

Rnd 3: Ch 1, **turn;** 🎥 work FPsc around first sc on Rnd 1 (*Fig. 15, page 47*), ch 5, (work FPsc around next sc on Rnd 1, ch 5) around; join with slip st to first sc: 6 ch-5 sps.

Rnd 4: Ch 1, turn; (sc, hdc, 3 dc, hdc, sc) in each ch-5 sp around; join with slip st to first sc: 6 petals.

Rnd 5: Ch 1, turn; work FPsc around first sc on Rnd 3, ch 7, (work FPsc around next sc on Rnd 3, ch 7) around; join with slip st to first sc: 6 ch-7 sps.

Rnd 6: Ch 1, turn; (sc, hdc, 5 dc, hdc, sc) in each ch-7 sp around; join with slip st to first sc, finish off.

Using photo as a guide for placement, sew Flower to Purse using long end.

If desired, using the Body as a pattern, make a lining and sew it in place around top edge.

Sleek Shawl

This little triangular shawl is perfect for dressy or casual wear.
The Crocodile Scales lie especially sleek in this design because the
Foundation Rows use treble crochet stitches instead of double crochets.

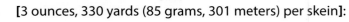 INTERMEDIATE

Finished Size:
14¹/₂" high x 56" long
(37 cm x 142 cm)

SHOPPING LIST

Yarn (Light Weight) 🧶 3

[3 ounces, 330 yards (85 grams, 301 meters) per skein]:

☐ 3 skeins

Crochet Hook

☐ Size H (5 mm) **or** size needed for gauge

GAUGE INFORMATION

In Crocodile Stitch,

    3 Scales = 4" (10 cm),

    10 rows = 2³/₄" (7 cm)

Gauge Swatch: 4" wide x 2" high

    (10 cm x 5 cm)

Work same as Shawl through Row 5: 3 Scales.

STITCH GUIDE

TREBLE CROCHET (*abbreviated tr*)

YO twice, insert hook in st indicated, YO and pull up a loop (4 loops on hook), (YO and draw through 2 loops on hook) 3 times.

The Shawl begins at the bottom point. Stitches are increased on the Foundation Rows.

INSTRUCTIONS

Ch 4; join with slip st to form a ring.

Row 1 (Wrong side)**:** Ch 3, 11 dc in ring to form first Scale; do **not** join.

Row 2 (Foundation row)**:** Ch 4 **(counts as first tr, now and throughout)**, do **not** turn; tr around post of last dc made on Row 1 *(Fig. 11a)*, ★ ch 2, dc in ring (center of Scale), ch 2, 2 tr around post of last dc *(Fig. 11b)*: 2 2-tr groups, 1 dc, and 2 ch-2 sps.

Fig. 11a

Fig. 11b

Row 3 (Scale row)**:** Ch 3 **(counts as first dc, now and throughout)**, work 5 dc down post of last tr made, rotate piece and work 6 dc up post of next tr to form a Scale *(Fig. 12)*, slip st in next dc, work 6 dc down post of next tr, rotate piece and work 6 dc up post of last tr: 2 Scales.

Fig. 12

Row 4 (Foundation row)**:** Ch 4, tr around post of last dc made, ch 2, dc in center of next Scale, ch 2, 2 tr in next slip st (between Scales), ch 2, dc in center of next Scale, ch 2, 2 tr around post of last dc: 3 2-tr groups, 2 dc, and 4 ch-2 sps.

Row 5 (Scale row)**:** Ch 3, work 5 dc down post of last tr made, rotate piece and work 6 dc up post of next tr, ★ slip st in next dc, work 6 dc down post of next tr, rotate piece and work 6 dc up post of next tr; repeat from ★ once **more**: 3 Scales.

Row 6 (Foundation row)**:** Ch 4, (tr, ch 2, dc) around post of last dc made, ch 2, (2 tr, ch 2, dc) in center of next Scale, ch 2, 2 tr in next slip st, ch 2, dc in center of next Scale, ch 2, 2 tr in next slip st, ch 2, (dc, ch 2, 2 tr) in center of next Scale, ch 2, (dc, ch 2, 2 tr) around post of last dc: 6 2-tr groups, 5 dc, and 10 ch-2 sps.

Row 7 (Scale row)**:** Ch 3, work 5 dc down post of last tr made, rotate piece and work 6 dc up post of next tr, ★ slip st in next dc, work 6 dc down post of next tr, rotate piece and work 6 dc up post of next tr; repeat from ★ across: 6 Scales.

Row 8 (Foundation row)**:** Ch 4, tr around post of last dc made, ch 2, dc in center of next Scale, ch 2, ★ 2 tr in next slip st, ch 2, dc in center of next Scale, ch 2; repeat from ★ across, 2 tr around post of last dc: 7 2-tr groups, 6 dc, and 12 ch-2 sps.

Row 9 (Scale row)**:** Repeat Row 7: 7 Scales.

Row 10 (Foundation row)**:** Ch 4, (tr, ch 2, dc) around post of last dc made, ch 2, (2 tr, ch 2, dc) in center of next Scale, ch 2, 2 tr in next slip st, ch 2, ★ dc in center of next Scale, ch 2, 2 tr in next slip st, ch 2; repeat from ★ across to last Scale, (dc, ch 2, 2 tr) in center of last Scale, ch 2, (dc, ch 2, 2 tr) around post of last dc: 10 2-tr groups, 9 dc, and 18 ch-2 sps.

Rows 11-34: Repeat Rows 7-10, 6 times: 34 2-tr groups, 33 dc, and 66 ch-2 sps.

Rows 35-49: Repeat Rows 7 and 8, 7 times; then repeat Row 7 once **more**: 41 Scales.

Row 50: Ch 4, 4 tr around post of last dc made, (dc, 6 tr, dc) in center of each Scale across, (4 tr, ch 4, slip st) around post of last dc; finish off.

We've created bonus videos for you @ www.leisurearts.com/6377

Take a look!

Perky Flower Motif

Unlike most Crocodile Stitch designs, the Scales in this motif are placed with the right side up, giving the petals an upward curve. The flirty flower lends itself to lots of projects, from scarves and cowls to blankets of all sizes. For ideas, see Things to Make with Motifs (page 44).

 **EASY**

Finished Size:
6¹/₂" (16.5 cm) square

SHOPPING LIST

Yarn (Medium Weight)

- ☐ Main Color (Off White) - 40 yards (36.5 meters)
- ☐ Contrasting Color (Pink) - 30 yards (27.5 meters)

Crochet Hook

- ☐ Size I (5.5 mm) **or** size needed for gauge

GAUGE INFORMATION

Gauge Swatch: 2³/₄" (7 cm) diameter
Work same as Motif through Rnd 2.

──── STITCH GUIDE ────

TREBLE CROCHET *(abbreviated tr)*
YO twice, insert hook in st or sp indicated, YO and pull up a loop (4 loops on hook), (YO and draw through 2 loops on hook) 3 times.

BEGINNING PUFF ST (uses one st)
★ YO, insert hook in st indicated, YO and pull up a loop even with loop on hook; repeat from ★ once **more**, YO and draw through all 5 loops on hook.

PUFF ST (uses one st or sp)
★ YO, insert hook in st or sp indicated, YO and pull up a loop even with loop on hook; repeat from ★ 2 times **more**, YO and draw through all 7 loops on hook.

THINGS TO MAKE WITH MOTIFS

This Motif can be used for many things. Make and sew 7 Motifs together to form a 45¹/₂" (115.5 cm) scarf, or make less for a cowl. You can make different sizes of blankets by whipstitching Motifs together *(Fig. 16a, page 47)*. Make 30 Motifs and sew 5 Motifs into 6 strips to make a baby blanket or lap robe that measures 32¹/₂" x 39" (82.5 cm x 99 cm). A full sized blanket can be made with 70 Motifs, sewing 7 Motifs into 10 strips, which will measure 45¹/₂" x 65" (115.5 cm x 165 cm).

INSTRUCTIONS

With Main Color, ch 5; join with slip st to form a ring.

Rnd 1 (Right side)**:** Ch 1, 8 sc in ring; join with slip st to first sc.

Note: Loop a short piece of yarn around any stitch to mark Rnd 1 as **right** side.

Rnd 2: Ch 3, work Beginning Puff St in same st as joining, ch 2, (work Puff St in next sc, ch 2) around; join with slip st to top of Beginning Puff St: 8 Puff Sts and 8 ch-2 sps.

Rnd 3: Slip st in first ch-2 sp, ch 1, 3 sc in same sp, ch 2, (3 sc in next ch-2 sp, ch 2) around; join with slip st to first sc, finish off: 24 sc and 8 ch-2 sps.

Rnd 4: With **right** side facing, join Contrasting Color with slip st in any ch-2 sp; ch 1, (sc, ch 6, sc) in same sp, ch 3, ★ (sc, ch 6, sc) in next ch-2 sp, ch 3; repeat from ★ around; join with slip st to first sc: 8 ch-6 sps and 8 ch-3 sps.

Rnd 5: ★ (5 Dc, ch 2, 5 dc) in next ch-6 sp (**Scale made**), working in **front** of next ch-3, slip st in center sc of next 3-sc group on Rnd 3 *(Fig. 13)*; repeat from ★ around; join with slip st to first dc: 8 Scales.

Fig. 13

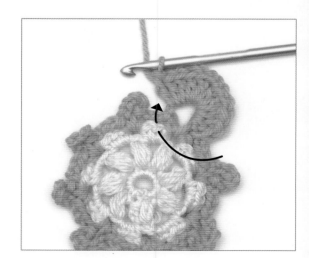

Rnd 6: Ch 1, **turn**; working in ch-3 sps on Rnd 4, ★ (2 sc, ch 8, 2 sc) in next ch-3 sp, ch 5; repeat from ★ around; join with slip st to first sc: 8 ch-8 sps and 8 ch-5 sps.

Rnd 7: Ch 1, turn; ★ working in **front** of next ch-5 sp and **behind** Scale, slip st in center of next ch-2 sp on Rnd 3 *(Fig. 14)*, ch 1, (6 dc, ch 2, 6 dc) in next ch-8 sp on previous rnd, ch 1; repeat from ★ around; join with slip st to first slip st, finish off: 8 Scales.

Fig. 14

Rnd 8: With **right** side facing and working in ch-5 sps on Rnd 6 **behind** Scales, join Main Color with slip st in any ch-5 sp; ch 2, (2 hdc, dc, tr) in same sp, (tr, dc, 3 hdc, dc, tr) in each ch-5 sp around, (tr, dc) in same sp as first st; join with slip st to top of beginning ch-2: 56 sts.

Rnd 9: Slip st in next hdc, ch 4, (tr, ch 3, 2 tr) in same st, dc in next 13 sts, ★ (2 tr, ch 3, 2 tr) in next hdc, dc in next 13 sts; repeat from ★ around; join with slip st to top of beginning ch-4: 68 sts and 4 corner ch-3 sps.

Rnd 10: Slip st in next tr and in next ch-3 sp, ch 3, work (Beginning Puff St, ch 3, Puff St) in same ch-3 sp, ch 1, skip next tr, ★ (work Puff St in next st, ch 1, skip next st) 8 times, work (Puff St, ch 3, Puff St) in next corner ch-3 sp, ch 1, skip next tr; repeat from ★ 2 times **more**, (work Puff St in next st, ch 1, skip next st) across; join with slip st to top of Beginning Puff St: 40 Puff Sts and 40 sps.

Rnd 11: Slip st in first corner ch-3 sp, ch 1, (2 sc, ch 2, 2 sc) in same sp, 2 sc in each ch-1 sp around working (2 sc, ch 2, 2 sc) in each corner ch-3 sp; join with slip st to first sc, finish off: 88 sc.

We've created bonus videos for you @ www.leisurearts.com/6377
Take a look!

GENERAL INSTRUCTIONS

ABBREVIATIONS

ch(s)	chain(s)
cm	centimeters
dc	double crochet(s)
FPsc	front post single crochet(s)
hdc	half double crochet(s)
mm	millimeters
Rnd(s)	Round(s)
sc	single crochet(s)
sp(s)	space(s)
st(s)	stitch(es)
tr	treble crochet(s)
YO	yarn over

SYMBOLS & TERMS

★ — work instructions following ★ as many **more** times as indicated in addition to the first time.

( ) or [ ] — work enclosed instructions **as many** times as specified by the number immediately following **or** work all enclosed instructions in the stitch or space indicated **or** contains explanatory remarks.

colon (:) — the number(s) given after a colon at the end of a row or round denote(s) the number of stitches or spaces you should have on that row or round.

CROCHET TERMINOLOGY	
UNITED STATES	INTERNATIONAL
slip stitch (slip st)	= single crochet (sc)
single crochet (sc)	= double crochet (dc)
half double crochet (hdc)	= half treble crochet (htr)
double crochet (dc)	= treble crochet(tr)
treble crochet (tr)	= double treble crochet (dtr)
double treble crochet (dtr)	= triple treble crochet (ttr)
triple treble crochet (tr tr)	= quadruple treble crochet (qtr)
skip	= miss

Yarn Weight Symbol & Names	LACE 0	SUPER FINE 1	FINE 2	LIGHT 3	MEDIUM 4	BULKY 5	SUPER BULKY 6
Type of Yarns in Category	Fingering, 10-count crochet thread	Sock, Fingering Baby	Sport, Baby	DK, Light Worsted	Worsted, Afghan, Aran	Chunky, Craft, Rug	Bulky, Roving
Crochet Gauge* Ranges in Single Crochet to 4" (10 cm)	32-42 double crochets**	21-32 sts	16-20 sts	12-17 sts	11-14 sts	8-11 sts	5-9 sts
Advised Hook Size Range	Steel*** 6,7,8 Regular hook B-1	B-1 to E-4	E-4 to 7	7 to I-9	I-9 to K-10.5	K-10.5 to M-13	M-13 and larger

*GUIDELINES ONLY: The chart above reflects the most commonly used gauges and hook sizes for specific yarn categories.

** Lace weight yarns are usually crocheted on larger-size hooks to create lacy openwork patterns. Accordingly, a gauge range is difficult to determine. Always follow the gauge stated in your pattern.

*** Steel crochet hooks are sized differently from regular hooks–the higher the number the smaller the hook, which is the reverse of regular hook sizing.

CROCHET HOOKS																
U.S.	B-1	C-2	D-3	E-4	F-5	G-6	7	H-8	I-9	J-10	K-10½	L-11	M/N-13	N/P-15	P/Q	Q	S
Metric - mm	2.25	2.75	3.25	3.5	3.75	4	4.5	5	5.5	6	6.5	8	9	10	15	16	19

GAUGE

Exact gauge is **essential** for proper size. Before beginning your project, make the sample swatch given in the individual instructions in the yarn and hook specified. After completing the swatch, measure it, counting your stitches and rows or rounds carefully. If your swatch is larger or smaller than specified, **make another, changing hook size to get the correct gauge.** Keep trying until you find the size hook that will give you the specified gauge.

FRONT POST SINGLE CROCHET

(abbreviated FPsc)

Insert hook from **front** to **back** around post of sc indicated *(Fig. 15)*, YO and pull up a loop, YO and draw through both loops on hook.

Fig. 15

WHIPSTITCH

With **wrong** sides together, sew through both pieces once to secure the beginning of the seam, leaving an ample yarn end to weave in later. Insert the needle from **back** to **front** through **both** loops of each stitch on **both** pieces *(Fig. 16a)*, **or** in end of rows *(Fig. 16b)*. Bring the needle around and insert it from **back** to **front** through the next stitch or strands on both pieces.

Continue in same manner, keeping the sewing yarn fairly loose.

Fig. 16a

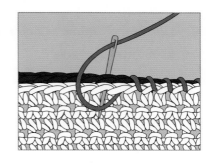

Fig. 16b

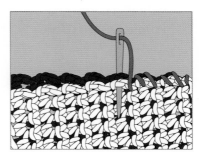

◼◻◻◻ **BEGINNER**	Projects for first-time crocheters using basic stitches. Minimal shaping.
◼◼◻◻ **EASY**	Projects using yarn with basic stitches, repetitive stitch patterns, simple color changes, and simple shaping and finishing.
◼◼◼◻ **INTERMEDIATE**	Projects using a variety of techniques, such as basic lace patterns or color patterns, mid-level shaping and finishing.
◼◼◼◼ **EXPERIENCED**	Projects with intricate stitch patterns, techniques and dimension, such as non-repeating patterns, multi-color techniques, fine threads, small hooks, detailed shaping and refined finishing.

YARN INFORMATION

The items in this book were made using Light Weight and Medium Weight yarns. Any brand of the specified weight of yarn may be used. It is best to refer to the yardage/meters when determining how many skeins or balls to purchase. Remember, to arrive at the finished size, it is the GAUGE/TENSION that is important, not the brand of yarn.

For your convenience, listed below are the yarns used to create our photography models.

SCALE BRACELET

Lion Brand® Vanna's Choice® Baby
#106 Little Boy Blue

FANCIFUL MITTS

Red Heart® Boutique Unforgettable™
Variegated - #3950 Petunia
Red Heart® Soft®
Purple - #3729 Grape

BORDERED SCARF

Lion Brand® Heartland®
#174 Joshua Tree

PLUSH PILLOW

Red Heart® Soft®
#9440 Light Grey Heather

LUXURIOUS COWL

Red Heart® Boutique Unforgettable™
#3945 Parrot

EMBELLISHED BAG

Lion Brand® Vanna's Choice®
Main Color - #302 Taupe Mist
Contrasting Color - #305 Pearl Mist

SLEEK SHAWL

Caron® Simply Soft® Light™
#0009 Hawaiian Sky

PERKY FLOWER MOTIF

Red Heart® Soft®
Main Color - #4601 Off White
Red Heart® Soft Baby Steps®
Contrasting Color - #9702 Strawberry